T0145036

Cody
and His Type 1 Diabetes:
Cody Gets an Insulin Pump and Continuous Glucose Monitor

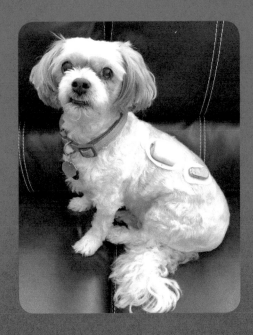

Amanda King
Author and Photographer

Archway Publishing books may be ordered through booksellers or by contacting:

Archway Publishing
1663 Liberty Drive
Bloomington, IN 47403
www.archwaypublishing.com
1 (888) 242-5904

Interior Image Credit: Amanda King

www.codyandt1diabetes.org
Special Thanks to Elm Point Animal Hospital

ISBN: 978-1-4808-8887-6 (sc)
ISBN: 978-1-4808-8889-0 (e)

Print information available on the last page.

Archway Publishing rev. date: 03/09/2020

Dedicated to my father, who always believed in me and taught me to never give up on my dreams.

This is Cody and he has Type 1 Diabetes.

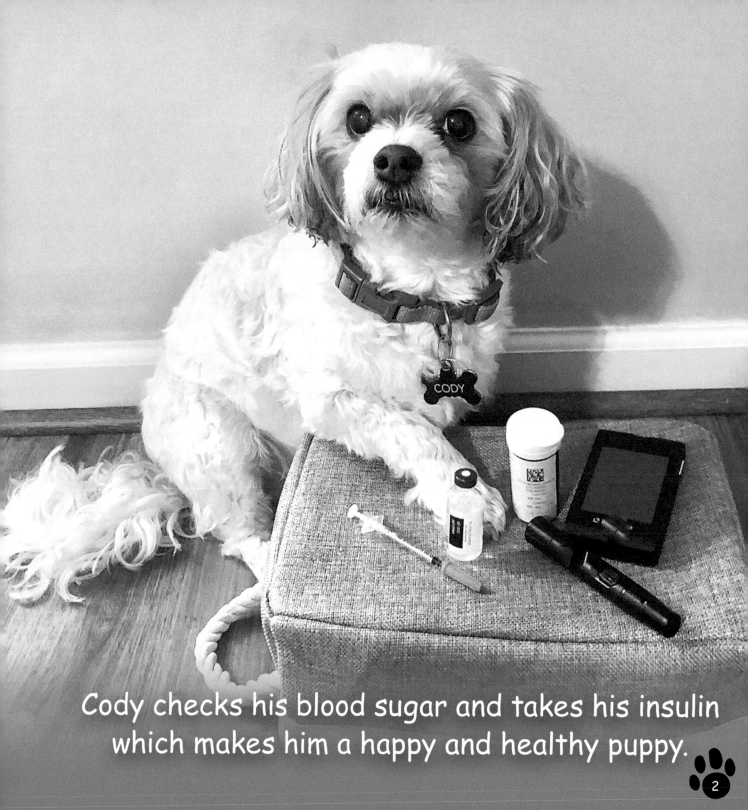

Cody checks his blood sugar and takes his insulin
which makes him a happy and healthy puppy.

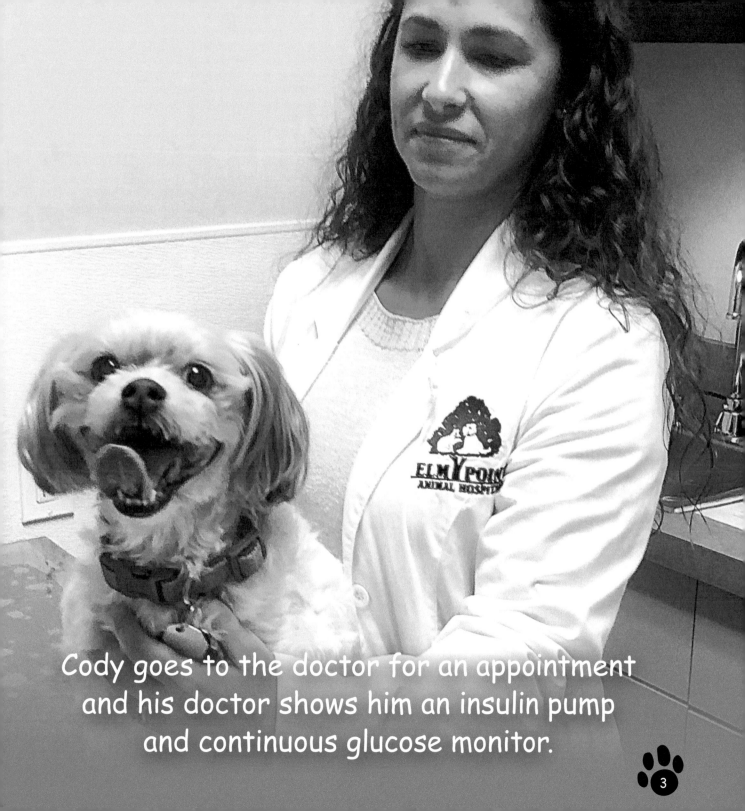

Cody goes to the doctor for an appointment and his doctor shows him an insulin pump and continuous glucose monitor.

Cody gets very excited when his doctor shows him how wearing the insulin pump can give him his insulin for 3 days with no shots.

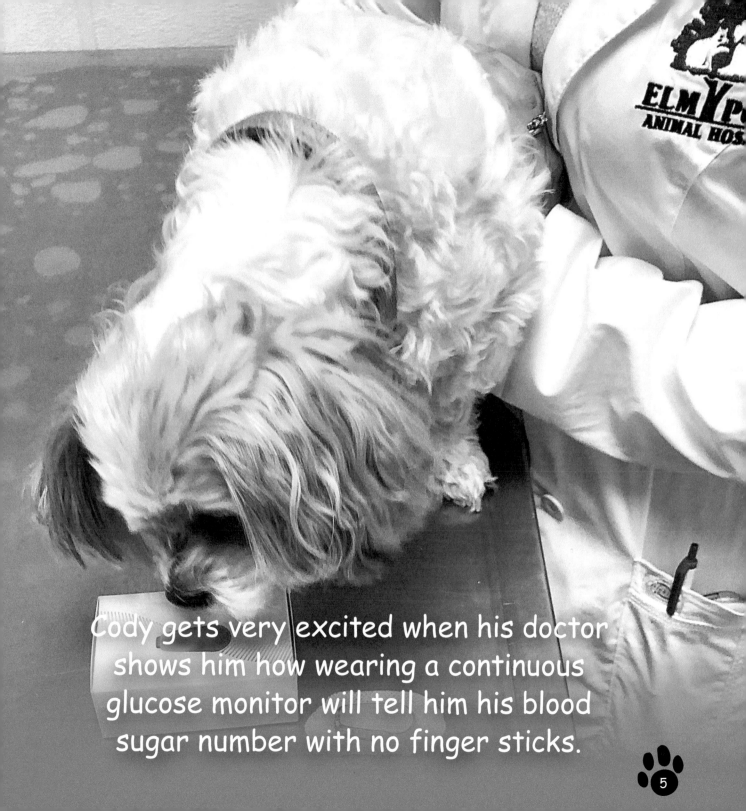

Cody gets very excited when his doctor shows him how wearing a continuous glucose monitor will tell him his blood sugar number with no finger sticks.

Cody and his doctor decide that an insulin pump and continuous glucose monitor are the best thing for Cody to help him with his Diabetes.

Cody waits by the mailbox for his insulin pump and continuous glucose monitor to get delivered.

Cody is on his way to see his doctor to learn how to use his new insulin pump and continuous glucose monitor.

Cody learns how to follow the directions on his insulin pump and fill it with insulin. He then sticks the pump on his skin and pushes the button.

Cody learns how to put on the glucose sensor and transmitter, then turn them on.

Cody loves his new insulin pump and continuous glucose monitor. He feels proud wearing them.

11

Cody can take a bath wearing them.

Cody can take a nap wearing them.

Cody can play in the snow wearing them.

Cody can play outside with his best friend Sammie while wearing them.

The most important thing of all is that
Cody is a brave, healthy, and happy
puppy and can still have fun!

16

Dear Parents,

When your child was diagnosis with Type 1 Diabetes, it was a scary time for both you and your child. These feelings are why my first book, *Cody and His Type 1 Diabetes*, was written and published. This book instantly became a useful and valuable tool for children with Type 1 Diabetes all over the United States and has reached as far as Australia, China, and United Kingdom. As technology is progressing with the way we manage our diabetes, I felt compelled to write and publish my second book, *Cody and His Type 1 Diabetes: Cody Gets an Insulin Pump and Continuous Glucose Monitor* . This book will help your child feel comfortable and proud, just like Cody, while they wear their own insulin pump and continuous glucose monitor.

Please visit www.codyandt1diabetes.org to view/purchase other products... Thank you!

                       Warm Thoughts,
                       Amanda King

The lovable main character is Cody, 12-year-old Shih Tzu Maltese Mix that became a part of the author's family at 8 weeks old. He loves to snuggle, play ball, go for rides in the car, and play with his best friend Sammie. Sammie is an 11-year-old Cockapoo that also became part of the author's family at 8 weeks old. Cody and Sammie are the author's biggest supporters and have been by her side through insulin shots, blood sugar checks, insulin pump site changes, glucose sensor changes, and so much more.

Please visit www.codyandt1diabetes.org to learn more about Cody.

"Mom I like this book. Cody is just like me and you and I'm happy with that!" Riley age 8, diagnosed April 2012.

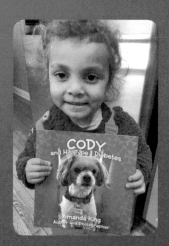

"I think Cody is so cute and I just love him, and I am so happy that the medicine makes him feel better so he can play!" Addison, age 3.

Printed in the United States
By Bookmasters